City Council Boston (Mass.).

Exercises at the Dedication of the Monument

To Colonel Robert Gould Shaw and the Fifty-Fourth Regiment of

Massachusetts Infantry, May 31, 1897

City Council Boston (Mass.).

Exercises at the Dedication of the Monument
To Colonel Robert Gould Shaw and the Fifty-Fourth Regiment of Massachusetts Infantry, May 31, 1897

ISBN/EAN: 9783337201555

Printed in Europe, USA, Canada, Australia, Japan

Cover: Foto ©ninafisch / pixelio.de

More available books at **www.hansebooks.com**

DEDICATION

OF THE

COLONEL ROBERT GOULD SHAW

MEMORIAL.

EXERCISES

AT THE

DEDICATION OF THE MONUMENT

TO

COLONEL ROBERT GOULD SHAW

AND THE

FIFTY-FOURTH REGIMENT OF MASSACHUSETTS INFANTRY,

MAY 31, 1897.

PUBLISHED BY ORDER OF THE CITY COUNCIL OF BOSTON.

BOSTON:
MUNICIPAL PRINTING OFFICE.
1897.

CITY OF BOSTON.

_____

IN COMMON COUNCIL, June 3, 1897.

Ordered, That the Superintendent of Printing, under the direction of the Committee on Printing, be directed to prepare and publish an edition of twenty-five hundred cloth bound copies of a volume containing an account of the services in connection with the unveiling of the SHAW MEMORIAL, the expense attending the same to be charged to the appropriation for City Council Incidental Expenses.

Passed. Sent up for concurrence.

IN BOARD OF ALDERMEN, June 8.

Concurred. Approved by the Mayor, June 10, 1897.

A true copy.

Attest:

JOHN T. PRIEST,
Assistant City Clerk.

CONTENTS

INSCRIPTIONS UPON THE
SHAW MONUMENT

UPON *the bronze an inscription taken by the artist from the seal of the Society of the Cincinnati of which Colonel Robert G. Shaw was a member:*

OMNIA·RELINQVIT
SERVARE·REMPVBLICAM

Underneath the main bronze:

·ROBERT·GOULD·SHAW·

COLONEL·OF·THE·FIFTY–FOURTH·REGIMENT·OF·MASSACHUSETTS
INFANTRY·BORN·IN·BOSTON·IO·OCTOBER·M·D·C·C·XXXVII
KILLED·WHILE·LEADING·THE·ASSAULT·ON·FORT·WAGNER
SOUTH·CAROLINA·I8·JULY·M·D·C·C·LXIII

Underneath, the verse of James Russell Lowell:

RIGHT·IN·THE·VAN·ON·THE·RED·RAMPART'S·SLIPPERY·SWELL
WITH·HEART·THAT·BEAT·A·CHARGE·HE·FELL
FOEWARD· AS · FITS · A · MAN
BUT · THE· HIGH · SOUL · BURNS · ON · TO· LIGHT · MEN'S · FEET
WHERE · DEATH · FOR · NOBLE · ENDS· MAKES · DYING · SWEET

CRISTIAN
MARTYR

9

Upon the back of the frame of the tablet the following inscription composed by Charles W. Eliot:

TO THE FIFTY-FOURTH   OF MASSACHUSETTS
REGIMENT   INFANTRY

THE WHITE OFFICERS
TAKING LIFE AND HONOR IN THEIR HANDS CAST IN THEIR LOT WITH MEN OF
A DESPISED RACE UNPROVED IN WAR AND RISKED DEATH AS INCITERS OF
SERVILE INSURRECTION IF TAKEN PRISONERS · BESIDES ENCOUNTERING
ALL THE COMMON PERILS OF CAMP MARCH AND BATTLE·

· THE BLACK RANK AND FILE
VOLUNTEERED WHEN DISASTER CLOUDED THE UNION CAUSE · SERVED
WITHOUT PAY FOR EIGHTEEN MONTHS TILL GIVEN THAT OF WHITE TROOPS·
FACED THREATENED ENSLAVEMENT IF CAPTURED · WERE BRAVE IN ACTION·
PATIENT UNDER HEAVY AND DANGEROUS LABORS · AND CHEERFUL AMID
HARDSHIPS AND PRIVATIONS·

TOGETHER
THEY GAVE TO THE NATION AND THE WORLD UNDYING PROOF
THAT AMERICANS OF AFRICAN DESCENT POSSESS THE PRIDE COURAGE
AND DEVOTION OF THE PATRIOT SOLDIER ·· ONE HUNDRED AND EIGHTY
THOUSAND SUCH AMERICANS ENLISTED UNDER THE UNION FLAG IN
M·D·C·C·C·LXIII — M·D·C·C·C·LXV

Underneath, upon the back of the terrace are the names of the five officers of the regiment who with Colonel Shaw were killed in battle or died while in the service:

CABOT·JACKSON·RUSSEL   WILLIAM·HARRIS·SIMPKINS
CAPTAIN   CAPTAIN

EDWARD·LEWIS·STEVENS   DAVID·REID
1ST LIEUTENANT   1ST LIEUTENANT

FREDERICK·HEDGE·WEBSTER
2ND LIEUTENANT

10

Immediately underneath these names is given an extract from the *address of Governor Andrew on the departure of the regiment:*

I·KNOW·NOT·MR·COMMANDER·WHERE·IN·ALL·HUMAN·HISTORY·TO·ANY
GIVEN·THOUSAND·MEN·IN·ARMS·THERE·HAS·BEEN·COMMITTED·A·WORK·AT
ONCE·SO·PROUD.SO·PRECIOUS·SO·FULL·OF·HOPE·AND·GLORY·AS·THE
WORK·COMMITTED·TO·YOU   GOVERNOR ANDREW

On the marble at one end of the terrace the words of Mrs. Waterston:

O·FAIR-HAIRED·NORTHERN·HERO··WITH·THY·GUARD·OF·DUSKY·HUE
UP·FROM·THE·FIELD·OF·BATTLE··RISE·TO·THE·LAST·REVIEW

On the marble at the other end of the terrace the words of Emerson:

STAINLESS·SOLDIER·ON·THE·WALLS··KNOWING·THIS·AND·KNOWS·NO·MORE
WHOEVER·FIGHTS·WHOEVER·FALLS··JUSTICE·CONQUERS·EVERMORE

UNVEILING OF THE SHAW MONUMENT

MAY 31, 1897

UNVEILING OF THE MONUMENT TO COLONEL ROBERT G. SHAW

CHIEF MARSHAL.
Francis H. Appleton.

ADJUTANT GENERAL
James T. Soutter.

HONORARY MILITARY STAFF
Colonel Charles F. Morse.
Colonel Robert H. Stevenson.
Colonel James Francis.
Major Henry L. Higginson.

MILITARY AIDS
(Members of Governor Wolcott's Staff)
Colonel Gordon Dexter,
    with 7th Regiment, N. G. S. N. Y., and 1st Cadets,
    M. V. M.
Colonel Edward B. Robins,
    with Battalion of Survivors.
Colonel Frank E. Locke,
    with United States Forces.
Colonel Richard D. Sears,
    with Massachusetts Volunteer Militia.

MOUNTED AIDS

George L. Peabody, *Chief.*

J. S. Russell.	R. E. Forbes.
W. Cameron Forbes.	D. H. Coolidge, Jr.
R. L. Agassiz.	R. S. Codman.
Copley Amory.	Alexander H. Ladd.
R. H. Hallowell.	Frank W. Hallowell.
Theodore Lyman, Jr.	T. P. Curtis.
T. G. Stevenson.	B. B. Crowninshield.
S. E. Courteney.	Henry A. Curtis.
F. H. Kennard.	George Francis Curtis.
Chester C. Rumrill.	Thomas E. Sherwin.
Robert Walcott.	Clement Morgan.
Alexander H. Higginson.	Edward W. Atkinson.
J. Bertram Read.	

AIDS IN MUSIC HALL

Elliot C. Lee, *Chief.*

J. Mott Hallowell.	Joseph Warren.
Hugh Williams.	John Warren.
J. Lowell Putnam.	Walter Briggs.

16

CEREMONIES

INCIDENT TO
THE UNVEILING OF THE

COLONEL ROBERT G. SHAW
MONUMENT

AT

MUSIC HALL, BOSTON, MONDAY, 31 MAY, 1897

❧

ORDER OF EXERCISES

MUSIC . . . . . *Patriotic Airs* . . . . Instrumental

MEETING called to order by the Chief Marshal, and the
Chairman of the Committee on the Monument
called to preside.

PRAYER . . . . Rev. Edward H. Hall, *Chaplain of the Day*

GREETING to His Excellency the Governor, Roger Wolcott, and Transfer of the Monument to His
Honor the Mayor of Boston, by the Chairman
of the Committee.

ADDRESS of His Excellency, Governor Wolcott, *Presiding Officer*

ACCEPTANCE by His Honor, Mayor Quincy.

CHORUS . . . . *"Our Heroes"*

ORATION . . . Prof. William James, *of Harvard University*

CHORUS . . . . *"Battle Hymn of the Republic"*

ADDRESS . Pres. Booker T. Washington, *of Tuskegee Institute*

MUSIC . . . . . . *America*✱ . . . . . Instrumental

✱All joined in singing the air.

CEREMONIES AT MUSIC HALL

SEATED upon the platform were the following guests: —

Gen. George L. Andrews.
Gen. F. H. Appleton.
Edward Atkinson.

Col. G. M. Barnard.
Hon. A. W. Beard.
Admiral Geo. E. Belknap.
Maj. George Blagden.
Maj. Louis Cabot.
Lieut. C. P. Clark, U. S. N.
Col. Charles R. Codman.
Capt. Henry N. Conrey.
Joseph A. Conry, *President Common Council.*
Lieut. James W. Cooke.
Lieut.-Gov. Crane.
Edward Parker Deacon.
Perlie A. Dyer, *Chairman Board of Aldermen.*
President Charles W. Eliot.
Col. J. M. Ellis.
William Endicott, Jr.
Col. W. H. Forbes.

Capt. John A. Fox.
Col. James Francis.
Hosea Gray.
Maj. J. C. Gray.
Col. Joseph W. Gelray.
Rev. Edward H. Hall.
Col. N. P. Hallowell.
Capt. Francis L. Higginson.
Col. H. L. Higginson.
Col. O. W. Holmes.
Capt. Edward H. Holt.
Surg. John Homans.
Col. Henry N. Hooper.
Col. Charles H. Hopper.
Col. Charles P. Horton.
Com. Howison, *Navy Yard.*
William Jackson, *City Engineer.*
Prof. William James, *Orator.*

M. P. Kennard.
Rt. Rev. William Lawrence.
Wm. P. Lawrence, *President of Senate.*
Col. Henry Lee.
John M. Little.
Col. Thomas L. Livermore.
Gen. Charles G. Loring.
Herbert Lyman.
Lieut. Wm. T. McAlpine.
Capt. Dennis Meehan.
Lieut. George W. Moore.
Col. C. F. Morse.
Col. T. L. Motley.
Gen. Robert S. Oliver.
George L. Osgood, *Leader of Chorus.*
Gen. John C. Palfrey.
Theodore K. Parker.
Gen. Charles L. Peirson.
Lieut. Richard Pendergast.
Capt. George Perkins, U. S. N.

Hon. E. L. Pierce.
Col. George Pope.
Mayor Josiah Quincy.
Col. A. A. Rand.
Gen. John H. Reed.
Capt. Morris P. Richardson.
Royal E. Robbins.
Col. Edward B. Robins.
John C. Ropes.
Col. Thomas Sherwin.
Maj. J. L. Stackpole.
Gen. Hazard Stevens.
Col. Robert H. Stevenson.
Augustus St. Gaudens.
Capt. Howard Stockton.
Col. Lincoln R. Stone.
Wilson B. Strong.
Brig.-Gen. Stryker.
J. L. Thorndike.
Hon. Winslow Warren.
Gen. Stephen M. Weld.
Governor Roger Wolcott.
Booker T. Washington.

REPORT

OF COLONEL HENRY LEE

ACTING CHAIRMAN

SHORTLY after 12.20 P. M., when the Germania Band had concluded several patriotic airs, the Chief Marshal, Francis II. Appleton, called to order those assembled, who more than filled the hall, and said : —

"I deem it a high honor to be permitted to call to order this vast and distinguished audience, myself a soldier of modern times in the presence of these veterans of war. I esteem it a further honor, and pleasure, to present to you as temporary Chairman, Colonel Henry Lee, Chairman of the Committee of Subscribers, and a member of our war Governor John A. Andrew's staff..

REPORT OF COLONEL HENRY LEE

ACTING CHAIRMAN

OU are too partial in calling me chairman of the committee. I wish the chairman, John M. Forbes, were here, — a man identified with Governor Andrew from the cold, chilly morning of preparation to the last review of the army in Washington. I say deliberately that there was no citizen of the Commonwealth who rendered more varied, more continuous, more valuable service during the war than John M. Forbes. To the State "his purse, his person, his extremest means lay all unlocked to her occasions." Unfortunately, old age has arrested him and prevented him from taking his place as chairman this morning.

Friends, more than twenty years ago the subscribers appointed a committee with full powers to procure a fitting testimonial to Col. Robert G. Shaw and his brave black soldiers. That committee has completed its task. It has invited the subscribers, the family and friends of the hero, with the remnant of his followers, some of his old comrades in arms, and all others interested, to listen to its final report, to look upon the memorial they have procured, to discharge the committee from further labors, and, if so minded, to crown them with approbation.

We ask your Excellency to preside on this occasion as the chief magistrate of the Commonwealth, and especially as the successor to our great war governor — the governor who was the first to prepare for war, the first to prepare for peace, the first to urge the policy of emancipation as a war measure, the first to insist upon the right and duty of the colored men to bear arms, feeling that not only the liberties of the colored men, but that the destinies of the country itself were involved in this question.

When, after two years' delay, the official sanction was granted, he hastened to organize regiments, to watch over them and contend for their rights, — promised and withheld.

" The monument," said Governor Andrew in his call for subscriptions, " is intended not only to mark the public gratitude to the fallen hero, who at a critical moment assumed a perilous responsibility, but also to commemorate that great event wherein he was a leader, by which the title of colored men as citizen soldiers was fixed beyond recall."

Time is wanting to detail the labors, anxieties, and disappointments, the weary delays encountered, the antipathy and incredulity of the army and the public at the employment of colored men as soldiers; the outrageous injustice of the Government to the colored soldiers even after the bloody assault on Fort Wagner, and the final triumph of the governor, only after a long legal struggle, and after he and his colored soldiers had passed through great anxiety and misery.

" I was opposed on nearly every side when I first favored the raising of colored regiments," said President Lincoln to General Grant, and no one can appreciate the heroism of Colonel Shaw and his officers and soldiers without adding to the savage threats of the enemy, the

24

disapprobation of friends, the antipathy of the army, the sneers of the multitude here, without reckoning the fire in the rear as well as the fire in front. One must have the highest form of courage not to shrink from such dismaying solitude.

As to the fallen hero who " had put on the crown of martyrdom," the governor had selected him, after deliberation, from a family consecrated to patriotism; had admired his heroism and was heartsick at his loss.

To express the universal grief at that loss and the appreciation of the great event in which he was a leader, this monument has been erected.

The State, through Governor Long, generously offered to the committee an admirable site for the monument, but upon examination this was declined lest the State House grounds should be disfigured. In this emergency the city came to our rescue, and not only furnished the ground, but made a liberal contribution of the terrace and framework of the monument. We therefore must turn to you, Mr. Mayor, and transfer to your Honor this precious memorial.

A generation has passed since this great work was contemplated. It is over twenty years since it was entrusted to the committee which I represent, and twelve years since it was confided to the sculptor, Mr. St. Gaudens. Two years was the time allotted for its completion. These two years have lengthened into twelve, a period of great anxiety for the committee lest they should not survive to accomplish their task, or, what was more important, lest the sculptor should be taken away, with his work unfinished. Those twelve years have been improved by the artist, whose inexorable conscience compelled him to prolong his labors at all hazards until his ideal should be realized.

Your Honor has witnessed the unveiling of the monument, and will, I am sure, congratulate us that, thanks to the sculptor, we have builded better than we knew.

No sweeter praise could be craved by any artist than the eulogy pronounced upon his work by the mother of the hero.

" You have immortalized my native city, you have immortalized my dear son, you have immortalized yourself."

ADDRESS

OF HIS EXCELLENCY ROGER WOLCOTT

GOVERNOR OF MASSACHUSETTS

ADDRESS OF HIS EXCELLENCY
ROGER WOLCOTT

GOVERNOR OF MASSACHUSETTS

M R. CHAIRMAN, Members of the Committee, Fellow-Citizens: I esteem it a signal honor and privilege to be called upon to bear part in these impressive services. We are met to commemorate not only a gallant, noble death, — not alone the gallant deaths of those who fell side by side with Col. Robert G. Shaw, — but we are here to commemorate an epoch in the history of a race.

On the blood-stained earthworks of Fort Wagner a race was called into sudden manhood. Even those whose hearts had yearned with the strongest sympathy and pity to the colored race had, up to that time, regarded as their leading characteristics a meek resignation, a patient submission to wrong. On that day the world learned to know that whatever the color of the skin, the blood that flowed in the veins of the colored man was red with the lusty hue of manhood and of heroism. When Abraham Lincoln, for the second time, took upon himself the great responsibility of the presidency, he spoke, in language that still thrills with a deep pathos and with lofty faith, the following words: " If God wills that this mighty scourge of war continue until all the wealth piled by the bondmen's two hun-

dred and fifty years of unrequited toil shall be sunk, and
until every drop of blood drawn with the lash shall be
paid by a drop of blood drawn with the sword, as was
said three thousand years ago, so still it must be said,
" The judgments of the Lord are true and righteous
altogether."

The great price was paid, — the price of heaped-up
treasure, the price of blood drawn from the veins of the
generous and gallant youth of the land.   But no heart
to-day, howsoever deeply wounded, can grudge that price.
Willingly and gladly it was given, and it is not with
sorrow, but with joy, that we commemorate the sacrifice.

And so it is with joyful and thankful hearts that we
remember the great deed which is to-day commemorated.
Sleep well, noble and heroic dead !   Live long, equally
noble and heroic survivors.   Like those who fell, you
held out your lives a sacrifice to country, and a grateful
nation treasures your act as a part of her undying fame.

The beautiful monument which we have witnessed
unveiled, in which the sculptor, with the hand of genius
seems to have caught, as if by inspiration, and to have
fixed in permanent bronze, the very spirit of that sacrifice — that monument becomes to-day the property of
the city of Boston.   I have the honor of presenting to
you His Honor Mayor Quincy.

ADDRESS

OF HIS HONOR JOSIAH QUINCY

MAYOR OF BOSTON

ADDRESS OF HIS HONOR, JOSIAH QUINCY
MAYOR OF BOSTON

YOUR Excellency, Ladies and Gentlemen: On this national aniversary, dedicated to the memory of those who died that their country might live, and that its free soil might no longer be trodden by the foot of any slave, we have our own especial commemoration of one of the most notable events in the history of Boston.

Thirty-four years ago, almost to the very day, our city witnessed the culmination of the anti-slavery agitation of which for a quarter of a century she had been the centre. Tongue and pen had here done their full work for human freedom; by other weapons and on other ground was the final issue to be determined. The time had come when the worthiness of men with black skins to bear arms and to be received into the fellowship of military service was to be put to the trial; when their courage and endurance were to be subjected to the supreme test of the battlefield. And the Commonwealth of Massachusetts — to her eternal honor — dared to entrust her white flag to their keeping, and to place one of her chivalry at their head. A negro regiment, the first raised by any Northern State, marched through our streets, bound for the front, with Robert G. Shaw in

command. The outward and visible sign of the enfran-
chisement of a race was here given when the fugitive
slave, transformed into a soldier by authority of a liberty-
loving State, went forth to bear his part in maintaining
the union of the nation and winning the freedom of his
people.

Two months later the answer to the question whether
the negro could fight and die for his country, like the
white man, came back, written in letters of blood, from
the ramparts of Fort Wagner; and a mighty army of
colored troops, no inconsiderable factor in the attainment
of the victory of the North, followed where Colonel Shaw
and the 54th Massachusetts had led the way.

A common trench in the soil of South Carolina, upon
the battle ground which has been well called the
Bunker Hill of the colored race, was the fitting sepulchre of white and black, of officer and private. To-day
we raise their monument, not over this far-off and
unmarked grave, but here upon the corner of Boston
Common, where began the march that ended for them
at Wagner. Facing the Capitol of the State in whose
service they were mustered in, on the spot where
Governor Andrew reviewed them and sent them forth
with the godspeed of the Commonwealth, we place this
memorial, — not as a mere likeness of the face and form
of Shaw, but as a monument to the soul of the regiment
which he led, as an expression of the great idea, of the
high purpose which called it into being.

Once more it marches to-day with full ranks, its survivors again passing through the streets which first knew
their martial tread a third of a century ago, the dead,
recalled to life by the genius of the sculptor, again
marching by the side of their heroic young commander.

" The rest," says the dying Hamlet, " is silence." Yet
from that silence beyond the grave — silence to us only

34

because our ears are not yet attuned to its harmonics — there come some living voices, repeating their message to generation after generation. Such, I think, will be the voice of Shaw, speaking through those closed lips of bronze. It is not often those whom the world esteems the most successful, or the greatest, who leave the most valuable examples and lessons to posterity. It is rather the man whose life or death touches some deep chord of universal sympathy, or appeals to the imagination or the sentiment of all mankind. When far greater soldiers are forgotten, our descendants will still cherish the memory of the gallant youth who fell "with his hurts before," leading a hopeless charge, blazing the path of freedom for a race in bondage.

Col. Henry Lee: On behalf of the city of Boston, I now gratefully accept the gift, precious alike as a memorial of the heroic dead and as a noble work of art, which you, on behalf of the committee which has so long had its execution in charge, have just placed in her keeping. May it stand in its place, telling its great and simple story, while this city shall stand. I extend to you, sir, who stood by the side of Governor Andrew, in whose great heart this regiment had its birth, at whose call Shaw assumed its command, my felicitations at having lived to see the dedication of this monument, which is in no small measure a memorial to the war governor whom you assisted in his great task.

I should fall short of my duty on this occasion if I failed also to express the thanks of the city to the sculptor, Augustus St. Gaudens, who has made the execution of this great work his chief concern through so many years, largely as a labor of love, and to congratulate him upon its more than successful completion. May the lesson which it teaches sink more deeply into the hearts

35

of our people as years go by. If they ever doubt as to the future of American political institutions, if they ever despair of the republic, may they here gather new inspiration and courage; may they here more fully realize that the country of freemen which was worth dying for a generation ago is worth living for now and hereafter. And let us here catch the forward step of the 54th Massachusetts, and serve, in whatever manner the peaceful opportunities of our time may permit, under the same glorious colors which it bore.

ORATION

BY PROFESSOR WILLIAM JAMES
OF HARVARD UNIVERSITY

GOVERNOR WOLCOTT: In that splendid charge at Fort Wagner, side by side with those to whom was given the happy destiny of an heroic death, were others, white and black, who like them gladly held out their lives a willing offering to Fate. Among these, wounded but not dead, fell Adjutant James. It is fitting that the committee should have selected his brother, Professor William James of Harvard University, to tell the story that is commemorated in this monument.

ORATION BY PROFESSOR WILLIAM JAMES

YOUR Excellency, your Honor, Soldiers and Friends: In these unveiling exercises the duty falls to me of expressing in simple words some of the feelings which have actuated the givers of St. Gaudens' noble work of bronze, and of briefly recalling the history of Robert Shaw and of his regiment to the memory of this possibly too forgetful generation.

The men who do brave deeds are usually unconscious of their picturesqueness. For two nights previous to the assault upon Fort Wagner, the 54th Massachusetts Regiment had been afoot, making forced marches in the rain; and on the day of the battle the men had had no food since early morning. As they lay there in the evening twilight, hungry and wet, against the cold sands of Morris Island, with the sea-fog drifting over them, their eyes fixed on the huge bulk of the fortress looming darkly three quarters of a mile ahead against the sky, and their hearts beating in expectation of the word that was to bring them to their feet and launch them on their desperate charge, neither officers nor men could have been in any holiday mood of contemplation. Many and different must have been the thoughts that came and went in them during that hour of bodeful reverie; but however free the flights of fancy of some of them may have been, it is improbable that any one who lay there had so wild and whirling an imagination as to foresee in prophetic vision this morning of a future May, when we, the people of a richer and more splendid Boston, with mayor and governor, and troops from other States, and every circumstance of ceremony, should meet together to celebrate their conduct on that evening, and do their memory this conspicuous honor.

How, indeed, comes it that out of all the great engagements of the war, engagements in many of which the troops of Massachusetts had borne the most distinguished part, this officer, only a young colonel, this regiment of black men and its maiden battle, — a battle, moreover, which was lost, — should be picked out for such unusual commemoration?

The historic importance of an event is measured neither by its material magnitude, nor by its immediate success. Thermopylæ was a defeat; but to the Greek imagination, Leonidas and his few Spartans stood for the whole worth of Grecian life. Bunker Hill was a defeat; but for our people, the fight over that breastwork has always seemed to show as well as any victory that our forefathers were men of a temper not to be finally overcome. And so here. The war for our Union, with all the constitutional questions which it settled, and all the military lessons which it gathered in, has throughout its dilatory length but one meaning in the eye of history. It freed the country from the social plague which until then had made political development impossible in the United States. More and more, as the years pass, does that meaning stand forth as the sole meaning. And nowhere was that meaning better symbolized and embodied than in the constitution of this first Northern negro regiment.

Look at that monument and read the story — see the

40

mingling of elements which the sculptor's genius has
brought so vividly before the eye. There on foot go the
dark outcasts, so true to nature that one can almost hear
them breathing as they march. State after State by its
laws had denied them to be human persons. The Southern leaders in congressional debates, insolent in their
security of legalized possession, loved most to designate
them by the contemptuous collective epithet of "this
peculiar kind of property." There they march, warm-
blooded champions of a better day for man. There on
horseback, among them, in his very habit as he lived,
sits the blue-eyed child of fortune, upon whose happy
youth every divinity had smiled. Onward they move
together, a single resolution kindled in their eyes, and
animating their otherwise so different frames. The
bronze that makes their memory eternal betrays the very
soul and secret of those awful years.

Since the 'thirties the slavery question had been the
only question, and by the end of the 'fifties our land lay
sick and shaking with it like a traveler who has thrown
himself down at night beside a pestilential swamp, and
in the morning finds the fever through the marrow of
his bones. " Only muzzle the Abolition fanatics," said the
South, " and all will be well again!" But the Abolition-
ists could not be muzzled, — they were the voice of the
world's conscience, they were a part of destiny. Weak
as they were, they drove the South to madness. " Every
step she takes in her blindness," said Wendell Phillips,
" is one more step towards ruin." And when South Carolina took the final step in battering down Fort Sumter,
it was the fanatics of slavery themselves who called upon
their idolized institution ruin swift and complete. What
law and reason were unable to accomplish, had now to
be done by that uncertain and dreadful dispenser of
God's judgments, War — War, with its abominably casual,

41

inaccurate methods, destroying good and bad together, , but at last unquestionably able to hew a way out of intolerable situations, when through man's delusion or perversity every better way is blocked.

Our great western republic had from its very origin been a singular anomaly. A land of freedom, boastfully so-called, with human slavery enthroned at the heart of it, and at last dictating terms of unconditional surrender to every other organ of its life, what was it but a thing of falsehood and horrible self-contradiction? For three quarters of a century it had nevertheless endured, kept together by policy, compromise, and concession. But at last that republic was torn in two; and truth was to be possible under the flag. Truth, thank God, truth! even though for the moment it must be truth written in hell-fire.

And this, fellow-citizens, is why, after the great generals have had their monuments, and long after the abstract soldier's-monuments have been reared on every village green, we have chosen to take Robert Shaw and his regiment as the subjects of the first soldier's-monument to be raised to a particular set of comparatively undistinguished men. The very lack of external complication in the history of these soldiers is what makes them represent with such typical purity the profounder meaning of the Union cause.

Our nation had been founded in what we may call our American religion, baptized and reared in the faith that a man requires no master to take care of him, and that common people can work out their salvation well enough together if left free to try. But the founders of the Union had not dared to touch the great intractable exception; and slavery had wrought and spread, until at last the only alternative for the nation was to fight or die. What Shaw and his comrades stand for and show us is that in

42

such an emergency Americans of all complexions and
conditions can go forth like brothers, and meet death
cheerfully if need be, in order that this religion of our
native land shall not become a failure on the earth.

We of this Commonwealth believe in that religion;
and it is not at all because Robert Shaw was an excep-
tional genius, but simply because he was faithful to it
as we all may hope to be faithful in our measure when
occasion serves, that we wish his beautiful image to stand
here for all time, an inciter to similarly unselfish public
deeds.

Shaw thought but little of himself, yet he had a personal charm which, as we look back on him, makes us
say with the poet: "None knew thee but to love thee,
none named thee but to praise." This grace of nature
was united in him in the happiest way with a filial heart,
a cheerful ready will, and a judgment that was true and
fair. And when the war came, and great things were
doing of the kind that he could help in, he went as a
matter of course to the front. What country under
heaven has not thousands of such youths to rejoice in,
youths on whom the safety of the human race depends?
Whether or not they leave memorials behind them,
whether their names are writ in water or in marble, depends mostly on the opportunities which the accidents HIGGINSON
of history throw into their path. Shaw recognized
the vital opportunity: he saw that the time had come
when the colored people must put the country in their
debt.

Colonel Lee has just told us something about the ob-
stacles with which this idea had to contend. For a large
party of us this was still exclusively a white man's war;
and should colored troops be tried and not succeed,
confusion would grow worse confounded. Shaw was a
captain in the Massachusetts Second, when Governor

43

Andrew invited him to take the lead in the experiment.
He was very modest, and doubted, for a moment, his own
capacity for so responsible a post. We may also imagine
human motives whispering other doubts. Shaw loved
the Second Regiment, illustrious already, and was sure of
promotion where he stood. In this new negro-soldier
venture, loneliness was certain, ridicule inevitable, failure
possible; and Shaw was only twenty-five; and, although
he had stood among the bullets at Cedar Mountain and
Antietam, he had till then been walking socially on the
sunny side of life. But whatever doubts may have beset
him, they were over in a day, for he inclined naturally
towards difficult resolves. He accepted the proffered
command, and from that moment lived but for one ob-
ject, to establish the honor of the Massachusetts 54th.

I have had the privilege of reading his letters to his
family from the day of April when, as a private in the
New York Seventh, he obeyed the President's first call.
Some day they must be published, for they form a veri-
table poem for serenity and simplicity of tone. He took
to camp life as if it were his native element, and (like so
many of our young soldiers) he was at first all eagerness
to make arms his permanent profession. Drilling and
disciplining; interminable marching and countermarch-
ing and picket-duty on the upper Potomac as lieutenant
in the Second Massachusetts Infantry, to which post he
had soon been promoted; pride at the discipline attained
by the Second, and horror at the bad discipline of other
regiments; these are the staple matter of the earlier letters, and last for many months. These, and occasional
more recreative incidents, visits to Virginian houses, the
reading of books like Napier's " Peninsular War " or the
" Idylls of the King," Thanksgiving feasts and races
among officers, that helped the weary weeks to glide away.
Then the bloodier business opens, and the plot thickens

44

till the end is reached. From first to last there is not a rancorous word against the enemy, — often quite the reverse, — and amid all the scenes of hardship, death, and devastation that his pen soon has to write of, there is unfailing cheerfulness and even a sort of innermost peace.

After he left it, Robert Shaw's heart still clung to the fortunes of the Second. Months later, when in South Carolina with the 54th, he writes to his young wife: "I should have been major of the Second now if I had remained there and lived through the battles. As regards my own pleasure, I had rather have that place than any other in the army. It would have been fine to go home a field officer in that regiment! Poor fellows, how they have been slaughtered!"

Meanwhile he had well taught his new command how to do their duty; for only three days after he wrote this he led them up the parapet of Fort Wagner, where he and nearly half of them were left upon the ground.

Robert Shaw quickly inspired others with his own love of discipline. There was something almost pathetic in the earnestness with which both the officers and men of the 54th embraced their mission of showing that a black regiment could excel in every virtue known to man. They had good success, and the 54th became a model in all possible respects. Almost the only trace of bitterness in Shaw's whole correspondence is over an incident in which he thought his men had been morally disgraced. It had become their duty, immediately after their arrival at the seat of war, to participate, in obedience to fanatical orders from the head of the department, in the sack and burning of the inoffensive little town of Darien on the Georgia coast. "I fear," he writes to his wife, "that such actions will hurt the reputation of black troops and of those connected with them.

45

For myself I have gone through the war so far without dishonor, and I do not like to degenerate into a plunderer and a robber, — and the same applies to every officer in my regiment. After going through the hard campaigning and the hard fighting in Virginia, this makes me very much ashamed. There are two courses only for me to pursue: to obey orders and say nothing; or to refuse to go upon any more such expeditions, and be put under arrest and probably court-martialed, which is a very serious thing." Fortunately for Shaw, the general in command of that department was almost immediately relieved.

Four weeks of camp life and discipline on the Sea Islands, and the regiment had its baptism of fire. A small affair, but it proved the men to be stanch. Shaw again writes to his wife: "You don't know what a fortunate day this has been for me and for us all, excepting some poor fellows who were killed and wounded. We have fought at last alongside of white troops. Two hundred of my men on picket this morning were attacked by five regiments of infantry, some cavalry, and a battery of artillery. The 10th Connecticut were on their left, and say they would have had a bad time if the 54th men had not stood so well. The whole division was under arms in fifteen minutes, and after coming up close in front of us, the enemy, finding us so strong, fell back. . . . General Terry sent me word he was highly gratified with the behavior of our men, and the officers and privates of other regiments praise us very much. All this is very gratifying to us personally, and a fine thing for the colored troops. I know this will give you pleasure, for it wipes out the remembrance of the Darien affair, which you could not but grieve over, though we were innocent participators."

The adjutant of the 54th, who made report of this

46

skirmish to General Terry, well expresses the feelings of loneliness that still prevailed in that command : —

"The general's favorite regiment," writes the adjutant,[1] "the 24th Massachusetts Infantry, one of the best that had so far faced the rebel foe, largely officered by Boston men, was surrounding his headquarters. It had been a living breathing suspicion with us — perhaps not altogether justly — that all white troops abhorred our presence in the army, and that the 24th would rather hear of us in some remote corner of the Confederacy than tolerate us in the advance of any battle in which they themselves were to act as reserves or lookers-on. Can you not then readily imagine the pleasure which I felt as I alighted from my horse, before General Terry and his staff — I was going to say his unfriendly staff, but of this I am not sure — to report to him, with Colonel Shaw's compliments, that we had repulsed the enemy without the loss of a single inch of ground. General Terry bade me mount again and tell Colonel Shaw that he was proud of the conduct of his men, and that he must still hold the ground against any future sortie of the enemy. You can even now share with me the sensation of that moment of soldierly satisfaction."

The next night but one after this episode was spent by the 54th in disembarking on Morris Island in the rain, and at noon Colonel Shaw was able to report their arrival to General Strong, to whose brigade he was assigned. A terrific bombardment was playing on Fort Wagner, then the most formidable earthwork ever built, and the general, knowing Shaw's desire to place his men beside white troops, said to him: "Colonel, Fort Wagner is to be stormed this evening, and you may lead the

---

[1] G. W. James: "The Assault upon Fort Wagner," in *War Papers read before the Commandery of the State of Wisconsin, Military Order of the Loyal Legion of the U. S.* Milwaukee, 1891.

column, if you say yes. Your men, I know, are worn
out, but do as you choose." Shaw's face brightened.
" Before answering the general, he instantly turned to
me," writes the adjutant, who reports the interview, " and
said, ' Tell Colonel Hallowell to bring up the 54th immediately.' "

This was done, and just before nightfall the attack
was made. Shaw was serious, for he knew the assault
was desperate, and had a premonition of his end. Walking up and down in front of the regiment, he briefly
exhorted them to prove that they were men. Then he
gave the order: " Move in quick time till within a hundred yards, then double quick and charge. Forward !"
and the 54th advanced to the storming, its colonel and
the colors at its head.

On over the sand, through a narrow defile which
broke up the formation, double quick over the chevaux
de frise, into the ditch and over it, as best they could,
and up the rampart; with Fort Sumter, which had seen
them, playing on them, and Fort Wagner, now one
mighty mound of fire, tearing out their lives. Shaw led
from first to last. Gaining successfully the parapet, he
stood there for a moment with uplifted sword, shouting
" Forward, 54th !" and then fell headlong, with a bullet
through his heart. The battle raged for nigh two hours.
Regiment after regiment, following upon the 54th,
hurled themselves upon its ramparts, but Fort Wagner
was nobly defended, and for that night stood safe. The
54th withdrew after two thirds of its officers and five
twelfths or nearly half its men had been shot down or
bayoneted within the fortress or before its walls. It was
good behavior for a regiment no one of whose soldiers
had had a musket in his hands more than 18 weeks,
and which had seen the enemy for the first time only
two days before.

48

"The negroes fought gallantly," wrote a Confederate officer, "and were headed by as brave a colonel as ever lived."

As for the colonel, not a drum was heard nor a funeral note, not a soldier discharged his farewell shot, when the Confederates buried him, the morning after the engagement. His body, half stripped of its clothing, and the corpses of his dauntless negroes were flung into one common trench together, and the sand was shoveled over them, without a stake or stone to signalize the spot. In death as in life, then, the 54th bore witness to the brotherhood of Man. The lover of heroic history could wish for no more fitting sepulchre for Shaw's magnanimous young heart. There let his body rest, united with the forms of his brave nameless comrades. There let the breezes of the Atlantic sigh, and its gales roar their requiem, while this bronze effigy and these inscriptions keep their fame alive long after you and I and all who meet here are forgotten.

How soon, indeed, are human things forgotten! As we meet here this morning, the Southern sun is shining on their place of burial, and the waves sparkling and the sea-gulls circling around Fort Wagner's ancient site. But the great earthworks and their thundering cannon, the commanders and their followers, the wild assault and repulse that for a brief space made night hideous on that far-off evening, have all sunk into the blue gulf of the past, and for the majority of this generation are hardly more than an abstract name, a picture, a tale that is told. Only when some yellow-bleached photograph of a soldier of the 'sixties comes into our hands, with that odd and vivid look of individuality due to the moment when it was taken, do we realize the concreteness of that bygone history, and feel how interminable to the actors in them were those leaden-footed hours and years. The

photographs themselves erelong will fade utterly, and
books of history and monuments like this alone will
tell the tale. The great war for the Union will be like
the siege of Troy, it will have taken its place amongst
all other " old, unhappy, far-off things and battles long
ago."

Ah, my friends, and may the like of it never be required of us again !

It is hard to end a discourse like this without one word
of moralizing; and two things must be distinguished in
all events like those we are commemorating, — the moral
service of them on the one hand, and on the other the
physical fortitude which they display. War has been
much praised and celebrated among us of late as a school
of manly virtue; but it is easy to exaggerate upon this
point. Ages ago, war was the gory cradle of mankind,
the grim-featured nurse that alone could train our savage
progenitors into some semblance of social virtue, teach
them to be faithful one to another, and force them to
sink their selfishness in wider tribal ends. War still ex-
cels in this prerogative; and whether it be paid in years
of service, in treasure, or in life-blood, the war tax is still
the only tax that men ungrudgingly will pay. How
could it be otherwise, when the survivors of one successful massacre after another are the beings from whose
loins we and all our contemporary races spring? Man
is once for all a fighting animal; centuries of peaceful
history could not breed the battle-instinct out of us; and
military virtue is the kind of virtue least in need of rein-
forcement by reflection, least in need of orator's or poet's
help.

What we really need the poet's and orator's help to
keep alive in us is not, then, the common and gregarious
courage which Robert Shaw showed when he marched
with you, men of the Seventh Regiment. It is that more

lonely courage which he showed when he dropped his
warm commission in the glorious Second to head your
dubious fortunes, negroes of the 54th. That lonely kind
of valor (civic courage as we call it in peace times) is the
kind of valor to which the monuments of nations should
most of all be reared, for the survival of the fittest has
not bred it into the bone of human beings as it has bred
military valor; and of five hundred of us who could storm
a battery side by side with others, perhaps not one would
be found ready to risk his worldly fortunes all alone in
resisting an enthroned abuse. The deadliest enemies of
nations are not their foreign foes; they always dwell
within their borders. And from these internal enemies
civilization is always in need of being saved. The nation
blest above all nations is she in whom the civic genius of
the people does the saving day by day, by acts without
external picturesqueness; by speaking, writing, voting
reasonably; by smiting corruption swiftly; by good temper between parties; by the people knowing true men
when they see them, and preferring them as leaders to
rabid partisans or empty quacks. Such nations have no
need of wars to save them. Their accounts with right-
eousness are always even ; and God's judgments do not
have to overtake them fitfully in bloody spasms and con-
vulsions of the race.

The lesson that our war ought most of all to teach us
is the lesson that evils must be checked in time, before
they grow so great. The Almighty cannot love such
long-postponed accounts, or such tremendous settlements.
And surely He hates all settlements that do such quan-
tities of incidental devils' work. Our present situation,
with its rancors and delusions, what is it but the direct
outcome of the added powers of government, the corrup-
tions and inflations of the war? Every war leaves such
miserable legacies, fatal seeds of future war and revolu-

tion, unless the civic virtues of the people save the State in time.

Shaw had both kinds of virtue. As he then led his regiment against Fort Wagner, so surely would he now be leading us against all lesser powers of darkness, had his sweet young life been spared. You think of many as I speak of one. For, North and South, how many lives as sweet, unmonumented for the most part, commemorated solely in the hearts of mourning mothers, widowed brides, or friends, did the inexorable war mow down! Instead of the full years of natural service from so many of her children, our country counts but their poor memories, " the tender grace of a day that is dead," lingering like echoes of past music on the vacant air.

But so and so only was it written that she should grow sound again. From that fatal earlier unsoundness those lives have bought for North and South together permanent release. The warfare is accomplished ; the iniquity is pardoned. No future problem can be like that problem. No task laid on our children can compare in difficulty with the task with which their fathers have to deal. Yet as we face the future, tasks enough await us. The republic to which Robert Shaw and a quarter of a million like him were faithful unto death is no republic that can live at ease hereafter on the interest of what they won. Democracy is still upon its trial. The civic genius of our people is its only bulwark, and neither laws nor monuments, neither battleships nor public libraries, nor great newspapers nor booming stocks ; neither mechanical invention nor political adroitness, nor churches nor universities nor civil-service examinations can save us from degeneration if the inner mystery be lost. That mystery, at once the secret and the glory of our English-speaking race, consists in nothing but two common habits, two inveterate habits carried into public life, — habits

so homely that they lend themselves to no rhetorical expression, yet habits more precious, perhaps, than any that
the human race has gained.   They can never be too often
pointed out or praised.   One of them is the habit of
trained and disciplined good temper towards the opposite
party when it fairly wins its innings; and the other, that
of fierce and merciless resentment towards every man or
set of men who overstep the lawful bounds of fairness or
break the public peace.

O my countrymen, Southern and Northern, brothers
hereafter, masters, slaves, and enemies no more, let us
see to it that both of those heirlooms are preserved.   So
may our ransomed country, like the city of the promise,
lie forever foursquare under Heaven, and the ways of all
the nations be lit up by its light.

ADDRESS

OF PRESIDENT BOOKER T. WASHINGTON,

OF TUSKEGEE INSTITUTE

GOVERNOR WOLCOTT: "One year ago, at the Commencement exercises of the oldest and most famous University of the western hemisphere, there was enacted a memorable scene. In the presence of hundreds of the Alumni of Harvard College, in the beautiful hall dedicated to those of her sons who gave their lives to their country's need, a colored man, born a slave, rose to receive an honorary degree at the hands of the President of the University. It was not the first time that a degree had been conferred upon one of his race. But in previous cases this distinction had been won by compliance with the requisite term of residence and by successfully passing certain academic examinations. In this case the honor was conferred because of wise leadership of his race, and of sagacious counsel to his countrymen, both white and black. As he ceased a speech that burned with restrained passion, and yet threw the calm, clear light of a tempered judgment upon the relations of the two races, that great audience was swept by wave after wave of enthusiastic applause. No man can more eloquently and wisely speak for the race which furnished the rank and file of the 54th Regiment than Booker T. Washington, of Tuskegee, Alabama."

ADDRESS OF
BOOKER T. WASHINGTON

R. CHAIRMAN, and Fellow-Citizens: In this presence, and on this sacred and memorable day, in the deeds and death of our hero, we recall the old, old story, ever old, yet ever new, that when it was the will of the Father to lift humanity out of wretchedness and bondage, the precious task was delegated to him who among ten thousand was altogether lovely, and was willing to make himself of no reputation that he might save and lift up others.

If that heart could throb and if those lips could speak, what would be the sentiment and words that Robert Gould Shaw would have us feel and speak at this hour? He would not have us dwell long on the mistakes, the injustice, the criticisms of the days

" Of storm and cloud, of doubt and fears
Across the eternal sky must lower
Before the glorious noon appears."

He would have us bind up with his own undying fame and memory, and retain by the side of his monument, the name of John A. Andrew, who, with prophetic vision and strong arm helped make the existence of the 54th Regiment possible ; and that of George L. Stearns, who, with hidden generosity and a great sweet heart, helped to turn the darkest hour into day, and in doing so freely gave service, fortune, and life itself to the cause which this day commemorates. Nor would he have us forget those brother officers, living and dead, who, by their baptism in blood and fire, in defense of union and freedom, gave us an example of the highest and purest patriotism.

To you who fought so valiantly in the ranks, the scarred and scattered remnant of the 54th Regiment, who with empty sleeve and wanting leg have honored this occasion with your presence, — to you your commander is not dead. Though Boston erected no monument, and history recorded no story, in you and the loyal race which you represent, Robert Gould Shaw would have a monument which time could not wear away.

But an occasion like this is too great, too sacred, for mere individual eulogy. The individual is the instrument, national virtue the end. That which was three hundred years being woven into the warp and woof of our democratic institutions could not be effaced by a single battle, as magnificent as was that battle; that which for three centuries had bound master and slave, yea, North and South, to a body of death, could not be blotted out by four years of war, could not be atoned for by shot and sword, nor by blood and tears.

Not many days ago, in the heart of the South, in a large gathering of the people of my race, there were heard from many lips praises and thanksgiving to God for his goodness in setting them free from physical slavery. In the midst of that assembly a Southern white man arose, with gray hair and trembling hands, the former owner of many slaves, and from his quivering lips there came the words: " My friends, you forget in your rejoicing that in setting you free God was also good to me and my race in setting us free." But there is a higher and deeper sense in which both races must be free than

58

that represented by the bill of sale. The black man who cannot let love and sympathy go out to the white man is but half free. The white man who would close the shop or factory against a black man seeking an opportunity to earn an honest living is but half free. The white man who retards his own development by opposing a black man is but half free. The full measure of the fruit of Fort Wagner and all that this monument stands for will not be realized until every man covered by a black skin shall, by patience and natural effort, grow to that height in industry, property, intelligence, and moral responsibility, where no man in all our land will be tempted to degrade himself by withholding from his black brother any opportunity which he himself would possess.

Until that time comes, this monument will stand for effort, not victory complete. What these heroic souls of the 54th Regiment began, we must complete. It must be completed not in malice, nor narrowness, nor artificial progress, nor in efforts at mere temporary political gain, nor in abuse of another section or race. Standing as I do to-day in the home of Garrison and Phillips and Sumner, my heart goes out to those who wore the gray as well as to those clothed in blue, to those who returned defeated to destitute homes, to face blasted hopes and shattered political and industrial system. To them there can be no prouder reward for defeat than by a supreme effort to place the negro on that footing where he will add material, intellectual, and civil strength to every department of state.

This work must be completed in public school, industrial school, and college. The most of it must be completed in the effort of the negro himself; in his effort to withstand temptation, to economize, to exercise thrift, to disregard the superficial for the real, the shadow for the substance, to be great and yet small; in his effort to

59

be patient in the laying of a firm foundation, to so grow
in skill and knowledge that he shall place his services in
demand by reason of his intrinsic and superior worth.
This, this is the key that unlocks every door of opportunity, and all others fail. In this battle of peace, the
rich and poor, the black and white may have a part.

What lesson has this occasion for the future? What
of hope, what of encouragement, what of caution?
"Watchman, tell us of the night, what the signs of
promise are." If through me, an humble representative,
nearly ten millions of my people might be permitted to
send a message to Massachusetts, to the survivors of the
54th Regiment, to the committee whose untiring energy
has made this memorial possible, to the family who gave
their only boy that we might have life more abundantly,
that message would be: Tell them that the sacrifice was
not in vain, that up from the depths of ignorance and
poverty we are coming, and if we come through oppres-
sion, out of the struggle we are gaining strength; by
way of the school, the well-cultivated field, the skilled
hand, the Christian home, we are coming up; that we
propose to invite all who will to step up and occupy this
position with us. Tell them that we are learning that
standing ground for a race, as for an individual, must be
laid in intelligence, industry, thrift, and property, not as
an end, but as a means to the highest privileges; that we
are learning that neither the conqueror's bullet, nor fiat
of law, could make an ignorant voter an intelligent voter,
could make a dependent man an independent man, could
give one citizen respect for another, a bank account,
a foot of land, or an enlightened fireside. Tell them
that, as grateful as we are to artist and patriotism for
placing the figures of Shaw and his comrades in physical
form of beauty and magnificence, that after all the real
monument, the greater monument, is being slowly but

60

safely builded among the lowly in the South, in the struggles and sacrifices of a race to justify all that has been done and suffered for it.

One of the wishes that lay nearest to Colonel Shaw's heart was, that his black troops might be permitted to fight by the side of white soldiers. Have we not lived to see that wish realized, and will it not be more so in the future? Not at Wagner, not with rifle and bayonet, but on the field of peace, in the battle of industry, in the struggle for good government, in the lifting up of the lowest to the fullest opportunities. In this we shall fight by the side of white men North and South. And if this be true, as under God's guidance it will that old flag, that emblem of progress and security which brave Sergeant Carney never permitted to fall upon the ground, will still be borne aloft by Southern soldier and Northern soldier, and in a more potent and higher sense we shall all realize that

> " The slave's chain and the master's
>   Alike are broken.
> The one curse of the races
>   Held both in tether :
> They are rising, — all are rising,
>   The black and white together ! "

Heroism in peacetime [handwritten annotation]

HISTORY OF THE SHAW MONUMENT

BY THE TREASURER OF THE FUND

HISTORY OF THE SHAW MONUMENT

BY THE TREASURER OF THE FUND

IN the autumn of 1865 a meeting was held in the council chamber at the State House, at the call of Governor Andrew, Dr. Samuel G. Howe, Senator Charles Sumner, Colonel Henry Lee, Mr. J. B. Smith, and others, to consider the matter of a suitable memorial to Robert G. Shaw, the late commander of the Massachusetts Fifty-fourth Regiment. The prime mover in this matter was doubtless the late Joshua B. Smith, a fugitive from slavery, who after his escape had been in the service of Colonel Shaw's family before he took the position of repute as the successful caterer, in which he became so well known in Boston. The purpose of the meeting was declared in the following words: —

"The monument is intended not only to mark the public gratitude to the fallen hero, who at a critical moment assumed a perilous responsibility, but also to commemorate that great event, wherein he was a leader, by which the title of colored men as citizen-soldiers was fixed beyond recall. In such a work all who honor youthful dedication to a noble cause and who rejoice in the triumph of freedom should have an opportunity to contribute."

I was not myself present at that meeting. A committee was appointed to carry this purpose into effect, consisting of John A. Andrew, chairman; Charles Sumner, Joshua B. Smith, Henry P. Kidder, Charles R. Codman, Henry W. Longfellow, James L. Little, William W. Clapp, Jr., Charles Beck, William G. Weld, Leonard A. Grimes, Royal E. Robbins, Robert E. Apthorp, Francis W. Bird, Edward W. Kinsley, George B. Loring, Alanson W. Beard, Solomon B. Stebbins, Robert K. Darrah; Charles W. Slack, secretary.

As I am informed, there had been some difference of opinion as to the kind of statue or memorial which should be procured. At the request of Senator Sumner I undertook to serve as the treasurer, with the understanding that my sole duty would be the custody of the funds. I believe that no one was ever asked to subscribe; all the contributions have been of a purely voluntary character, most gladly given. Within the next two or three months after the meeting the sum of three thousand one hundred and sixty-one dollars ($3161) had been placed in my hands.

The death of Governor Andrew soon after occurred, and later several of the chief promoters of this memorial, including Senator Sumner, passed away. The interest in the subject appeared to have ceased for the moment.

In 1876 the fund had reached a little over seven thousand dollars ($7000) by investment and reinvestment.

As there appeared to be no effective committee in charge of this matter, and believing that a small, well-chosen committee would be more likely to act in a judicious manner than a large one, the suggestion was made to all the subscribers to appoint Messrs. John M. Forbes, Henry Lee, and Martin P. Kennard as such committee, and their written assent and approval were obtained thereto.

Some previously unpaid subscriptions were then called

66

in and several additional subscriptions were volunteered, so that the total amount actually received from subscribers was raised a trifle over seventy-five hundred dollars ($7521). The names of the subscribers were as follows:

George C. Ward, Mrs. Lydia Jackson, Hon. Charles Sumner, Mrs. John E. Lodge, N. Livermore & Son, Mrs. Maria Weston Chapman, William G. Weld, Samuel G. Ward, S. N. Havens, John Fenno Tudor, Henry Sturgis Grew, and George O. Hovey, of Boston, Mass.; Richard Warren Weston, Horace Gray, Lucius Tuckerman, Edward F. Davison, Daniel C. Bacon, and Robert B. Minturn, of New York, N. Y.; F. J. Child, Robert B. Storer, James Russell Lowell, and Charles E. Norton, of Cambridge, Mass.; Edward Atkinson, Henry Lee, and Martin P. Kennard, of Brookline, Mass.; Alexander H. Bullock and Ichabod Washburn, of Worcester, Mass.; Samuel May, Jr., and Mrs. J. C. Gunn, of Leicester, Mass.; Zenas M. Crane, of Dalton, Mass.; John M. Forbes, of Milton, Mass.; Edmund Tweedy, of Milwaukee, Wis.; Robert Ferguson, of Morton, Carlisle, England.

In 1883 the fund having reached nearly seventeen thousand dollars ($17,000), it seemed to be time to move for the execution of the work. A desire had been expressed to me by Senator Sumner that the work should consist of a statue of Colonel Shaw mounted, in very high relief upon a large bronze tablet.

A suitable place for such a work seemed to be in the curve on the front of the State House where a tablet of moderate size could be placed in the wall, rising a little above it with a seat at the level of the sidewalk. Application was made through Governor Long, with his hearty approval, for a right to place the tablet at this point if such a work should be executed, and was cheerfully granted.

Happening to call upon my neighbor and friend, the late H. H. Richardson, he desired to know what action had been taken, if any, having a great personal interest in his memory of Colonel Shaw and being desirous that the work should be one of highest merit. On the submission of the plan for an alto-relievo in front of the State House, he gave his most earnest assent, offering his services to do the architectural work and suggesting Augustus St. Gaudens as the sculptor, whose statue of Admiral Farragut had so lately called attention to his great skill.

It was then suggested to the committee that the surest way to carry out our plans would be to select an artist without confusing ourselves with any competition. The contract was accordingly made with Mr. St. Gaudens on February 23, 1884, in the hope and expectation that an alto-relievo suitable to the place chosen would be put in position in two years. But as Mr. St. Gaudens dealt with the subject it grew upon him in its importance, and with that conscientious spirit which marks the true artist he has devoted the better part of twelve years to constant thought and work upon his grand design.

As the artist's conception developed, the size of the panel became too great for the space originally chosen. The suggestion was then made by the late Arthur Rotch to place it on the Common between the two great trees where it now stands.

Mr. Charles F. McKim, the architect who succeeded Mr. Richardson as the artist's adviser, had become greatly interested in the matter and had volunteered his services for the architectural work. How great this service had been could not become apparent until the unveiling. Suffice it that the architectural design is on the high plane of the bronze tablet which it sustains. His admirable design having been sketched, an application was

68

made by Mr. George von L. Meyer, then an alderman of the city of Boston, for an appropriation on the part of the city for the construction of the terrace and stone work in which the bronze tablet has now been placed upon the Common. With judicious liberality a contract was made by the City Government with Norcross Brothers for the execution of this work, at a cost of nearly twenty thousand dollars ($20,000).

In this long interval, the funds which were placed on deposit in the New England Trust Company as soon as the contract had been made have gradually accumulated, until the original subscriptions of a little over seventy-five hundred dollars ($7521) will yield nearly twenty-three thousand dollars ($23,000). But even then, when the artist shall have paid the heavy cost of casting in bronze, and also paid for all the necessary skilled work required in preparing for the founder, he may secure to his own use and benefit only the fair day's wages of a good stonecutter or stucco worker for the time which during the term he has devoted to this the great effort of his lifetime. Even that is doubtful, because with that conscientious determination to have everything right and suitable he has felt compelled to change in some respects the design of the marble frame and the form of the lettering, so that there may be extra charges incurred by his orders to the amount of two thousand or three thousand dollars ($3000) in the construction of the terrace and the marble framework above the contract, which perhaps it will be suitable for the city to defray in view of the credit and honor which is sure to come to Boston in the possession of such an imperishable work.

It is not often that one who has no artistic aptitude comes into such close relation with the evolution of a monument. Had I the right knowledge of technical terms, I should be inclined to give a little account of my

69

observations during the progress of this memorial. Few persons can have the slightest conception of the energy which a great artist must expend, not only in the conception of the work itself, but in the actual effort, physical, mechanical, and manual, which is necessary to bring that conception into imperishable bronze; the amount of work required from skilled workmen under the supervision of the artist in the process of converting his own conception from the clay model, first into plaster, then into the mould, and lastly, into the bronze, is something of which the writer for one had no previous conception.

For the rest, the work will speak for itself. The committee and the treasurer alike sometimes feared that the artist might not live long enough to complete this great work. Now that it is done, and that they themselves will have the satisfaction of placing it in the custody of the city and the State, they feel that they will have been fully justified and that their method of procuring this monument may be approved.

Of the twenty-one members of the original committee appointed to take action in the matter, but four now survive.

Among the misgivings of the treasurer while watching the progress of this work in the mere process of manufacture had been the fear that so extensive and difficult a casting might fail in its execution; but when the contract was made with the Gorham Manufacturing Company, his anxiety was almost wholly removed, and his previous fears have proved to be without cause.

Some exceptions have been taken to the decision of the committee to have the addresses made in the Music Hall rather than at the monument itself; but after full consideration of the matter, and in view of the present condition of the State House and the grounds, there seemed to be no alternative. The space which would

70

have remained available for those who have the direct and most personal interest in this matter, after providing for officials and for the passing of the military at the monument, was found to be wholly insufficient for any suitable arrangements in the open air.

The committee and the treasurer, representing the subscribers, have been placed by the circumstances of the case in the position of hosts, inviting the authorities of the city, the State, and other guests to be present at the unveiling of the monument. The writer may be permitted to say that most careful supervision has been given, especially by Colonel Lee, to the distribution of the tickets to the hall, to the end that no one might be forgotten who had even a remote claim to be present; yet it may happen that some have been overlooked.

The committee requested General Francis H. Appleton, of the governor's staff, to act as chief marshal, and to his most effective preparation are due the excellent arrangements for the military parade on Decoration Day and for caring for the guests in the hall.

It is in order that those who were present may have knowledge of all the facts and of the names of the subscribers, so few of whom are living, that this statement is now submitted.

The service of Mr. John B. Seward should be recognized; he has kept the accounts and held supervision over all matters connected with the trust, in order that there might be no confusion in case of accident to the undersigned.

EDWARD ATKINSON,
Treasurer Shaw Monument Fund.

BOSTON, May 22, 1897.

71

/

www.ingramcontent.com/pod-product-compliance
Lightning Source LLC
Chambersburg PA
CBHW020244090426
42735CB00010B/1834

*9 7 8 3 3 3 7 2 0 1 5 5 5 *